Fronteras Americanas

Contents

Foreword

When my family came to Canada, the designation for us was displaced persons, usually shortened to DPs and often alliteratively decorated with "dirty." Other decades have produced their own formulations of national otherness: immigrants and foreigners, refugees and aliens, newcomers and new Canadians. Terminology apart, these people's journeys are all different and all the same. *Fronteras Americanas* is a vivid and arresting theatre piece drawn from its creator's own singular migration. But Guillermo Verdecchia both de-constructs and re-constructs the model in his personal meditation on displacement, and indeed, in his celebration of it.

Guillermo Verdecchia's own origins are Latin, and his agenda here is the investigation of the Latino stereotypes and received notions that get in the way of true perception. The playwright's dossier overflows with devastating data from pop culture, tourist guides, life-style journalism, commercials, advertising and supermarket shelves. Historical briefings and quizzes and lectures—both mock and unmoving-eyeball serious—share the platform with audio and visual samples. He annotates furiously, flicking political, historical, linguistic, musical, moral, sexual, even

Terpsichorean, challenges at us as we scramble to gain a foothold in his demanding new topography. His range of references is vast and truly pan-American: Federico García Lorca and Ricky Ricardo, made-for-TV drug-cartel movies and Carlos Fuentes, the Zoot Suit Riots and "Chico and the Man," Astor Piazzolla and Speedy Gonzalez, Free Trade and Simón Bolívar, Eva Perón and the Frito Bandito. Just as rejoicing in diversities forms the basis of the work's content, so, too, diversity is the guiding principle of its form.

The broad range of the playwright's dramatic territory is held together by the tension at the heart of his discourse: the dialogue between his two stage personae, "Verdecchia" and "Wideload" (a.k.a. Facundo Morales Segundo). Together these two weave the many narrative, reflective, dialectic and personal strands of *Fronteras Americanas*. "Wideload," an inflated stereotype designed to deflate stereotypes, is a shrewdly witty commentator. He ponders "Saxonian" attitudes, turns Latino clichés on their sombreros, and even challenges the play itself, offering dramaturgy and criticism from inside the action. He is both a lit match and a safety curtain for the more volatile range of "Verdecchia," and there are no prizes for guessing who *he* is. "Verdecchia's" reflections move from humiliation at the hands of both education and entertainment systems to the shock and horror of what he experiences on his return to South America. Through "Verdecchia," the playwright extends his grasp to the poetic—in the emotional meaning beneath the tango's angularity—and to the mystical—in his spiritual search for integration.

Fronteras Americanas is dazzlingly animated by Guillermo Verdecchia's intelligence, wit and curiosity. But the satiric, the sardonic and the ironic are all counterweighted by the extraordinary personal candour of the writing. It is here—in Guillermo Verdecchia's brave commitment to the truth of "Verdecchia"—that the work opens up and absorbs common experiences. Displacement is his theme, with many variations: displacement from one's history, from one's past, from one's surroundings, from oneself. Telling his story, the playwright tells all our stories. How we are torn apart by the conflicting impulses to belong and to remain separate. How we allow ourselves to yield to the same suspicion with which we have been treated. How we want to both stand out and disappear. How we betray ourselves, giving away our very *names* for the quick trade-off of pronunciation ease and acceptance. How we flirt with self-hatred through our fears ("I know that somewhere in my traitorous heart I can't stand people I claim are my brothers").

Guillermo Verdecchia's struggle towards his self shapes the dramatic movement of *Fronteras Americanas:* it is the border within himself that must be crossed. Like all true artists, he embraces the paradox. He takes us with him: "And you? Did you change your name somewhere along the way? Does a part of you live hundreds or thousands of kilometres away? Do you have two countries, two memories? Do you have a border zone?" He urges a new geography of the mind and spirit, quoting Octavio Paz: "I am not at the crossroads / to choose / is to go wrong." If uncontrolled displacement was the pattern of the past, *willed* displacement will be the remedy of the future.

Urjo Kareda, July 1993

Preface

Fronteras Americanas began as a long letter to a close friend that I wrote during a trip to Argentina in 1989. Re-reading it—I made a copy of it for some mysterious reason—I found that hidden beneath the travelogue were some intensely personal questions that I had been struggling with for some time but which I could only now begin to articulate. In an attempt to better understand those questions I began to read, reflect and write.

Fronteras Americanas makes no claim to be the definitive explanation of the Latin experience in North America, or the immigrant experience, or anything of that nature. Our experiences on this continent are too varied, too fantastic to ever be encompassed in any single work. *Fronteras Americanas* is part of a process, part of a much larger attempt to understand and to invent. As such, it is provisional, atado con alambre. In performance, changes were made nightly depending on my mood, the public, our location, the arrangement of the planets .... I hope that anyone choosing to perform this text will consider the possibilities of making (respectful) changes and leaving room for personal and more current responses.

Many people have had a hand in shaping this play and I am most grateful to them: my good friend Damon D'Oliveira, whose hysterical improvisations, direct responses to the bad television shows we often auditioned for, helped bring Facundo a.k.a. Wideload to life; Janette and Doug Pirie, who lodged me and lent me clothes; Urjo Kareda and everyone at the Tarragon; Peter Hinton, Iris Turcott and Candace Burley at Canadian Stage; the Ontario Arts Council, the Canada Council; and of course, Tamsin, who put up with me while I wrote it.

The play was further refined by the gentle and intelligent dramaturgy of Jim Warren and by those generous audience members who came to listen and stayed to share their border stories.

Guillermo Verdecchia, July 1993

Fronteras Americanas

Fronteras Americanas was first produced at the Tarragon Theatre Extra Space in January 1993.

Directed by Jim Warren
Designed by Glenn Davidson
Stage Managed by Season Osborne
Performed by Guillermo Verdecchia

It was subsequently performed at the Festival des Amériques in Montreal in June 1993, where it was stage managed by William Gosling, and remounted at the Tarragon Theatre Main Space in October 1993.

Act I

As the audience enters, James Blood Ulmer's Show Me Your Love (America) *plays. Two slides are projected*

SLIDE It is impossible to say to which human family we belong. We were all born of one mother America, though our fathers had different origins, and we all have differently coloured skins. This dissimilarity is of the greatest significance.
— Simón Bolívar

SLIDE Fronteras. Borders. Americanas. American.

Welcome

[VERDECCHIA *enters*]

VERDECCHIA Here we are. All together. At long last. Very exciting. I'm excited. Very excited.
    Here we are.

SLIDE Here We Are

    Now because this is the theatre when I say we I

mean all of us and when I say here I don't just mean
at the Tarragon, I mean America.

SLIDE Let us compare geographies

And when I say AMERICA I don't mean the
country, I mean the continent. Somos todos
Americanos. We are all Americans.

Now—I have to make a small confession—I'm
lost. Somewhere in my peregrinations on the continent, I lost my way.

Oh sure I can say I'm in Toronto, at 30 Bridgman
Avenue, but I don't find that a very satisfactory
answer—it seems to me a rather inadequate descrip-
tion of where I am.

Maps have been of no use because I always forget that they are metaphors and not the territory; the
compass has never made any sense—it always spins
in crazy circles. Even gas-station attendants haven't
been able to help; I can never remember whether it
was a right or a left at the lights and I always miss
the exits and have to sleep by the side of the road or
in crummy hotels with beds that have Magic Fingers
that go off in the middle of the night.

So, I'm lost and trying to figure out where I took
that wrong turn … and I suppose you must be lost
too or else you wouldn't have ended up here, tonight.

I suspect we got lost while crossing the border.

SLIDE Make a run for the border / Taco Bell's got your order

The Border is a tricky place. Take the

Latin–North American border.

SLIDE map of the Mexico–U.S. border

Where and what exactly is the border? Is it this
line in the dirt, stretching for 3,000 kilometres? Is the
border more accurately described as a zone which
includes the towns of El Paso and Ciudad Juárez? Or
is the border—is the border the whole country, the
continent? Where does the U.S. end and Canada
begin? Does the U.S. end at the 49th parallel or does
the U.S. only end at your living room when you
switch on the CBC? After all, as Carlos Fuentes
reminds us, a border is more than just the division
between two countries; it is also the division between
two cultures and two memories.[1]

SLIDE Remember the Alamo?

The Atlantic has something to say about the
border: "The border is transient. The border is
dangerous. The border is crass. The food is bad, the
prices are high, and there are no good bookstores. It
is not the place to visit on your next vacation."[2]

To minimize our inconvenience, I've hired a
translator who will meet us on the other side.

The border can be difficult to cross. We will have
to avoid the Border Patrol and the trackers who cut
for sign. Some of you may wish to put carpet on the
soles of your shoes, others may want to attach cow's
hooves to your sneakers. I myself will walk backwards
so that it looks like I'm heading north.

Before we cross please disable any beepers, cellular phones or fax machines and reset your watches to border time. It is now Zero Hour.

El Bandito

[*Music:* Aquí vienen los Mariachi]

SLIDE Warning

SLIDE Gunshots will be fired in this performance

SLIDE Now

[*Gunshots. The performer appears wearing bandito outfit. He has shifted into his other persona,* WIDELOAD]

WIDELOAD Ay! Ayayayay! Aja. Bienvenidos. Yo soy el
mesonero acá en La Casa de La Frontera. Soy el guía.
A su servicio. Antes de pasar, por favor, los latinos se
pueden identificar? Los "latinoamericanos" por favor
que pongan las manos en el aire … [*he counts*] Que
lindo … mucho gusto … Muy bien. Entonces el
resto son … gringos. Lo siguiente es para los gringos:
Eh, jou en Méjico now. Jou hab crossed de border. Why? What you lookin' for? Taco Bell nachos
wif "salsa sauce," cabrón? Forget it gringo. Dere's no
pinche Taco Bell for thousands of miles. Here jou eat
what I eat and I eat raw jalopeño peppers on dirty,
burnt tortillas, wif some calopinto peppers to give it
some flavour! I drink sewer water and tequila. My

22

breath keells small animals. My shit destroys lakes.
Jou come dis far south looking for de authentic
Méjico? Jou looking for de real mezcal wit de real
worm in it? I'll show you de real worm—I'll show jou
de giant Mexican trouser snake. I will show you fear
in a handful of dust ...

Jou wrinklin' jour nose? Someting stink? Somebody smell aroun' here? Si, I esmell. I esmell because
I doan bathe. Because bad guys doan wash. Never.

Bandito maldito, independista, Sandinista,
Tupamaro, mao mao powpowpow.

[WIDELOAD *removes bandito outfit*]

Ees an old Hallowe'en costume. Scary huh?

Introduction to Wideload

WIDELOAD Mi nombre es Facundo Morales Segundo.
Algunos me llaman El Tigre del Barrio. También me
dicen El Alacran ...

[*Music:* La Cumbia Del Facundo, *Steve Jordan*]

My name ees Facundo Morales Segundo. Some
of you may know me as de Barrio Tiger. I am a direct
descendant of Túpac Amaru, Pancho Villa, Doña
Flor, Pedro Navaja, Sor Juana and Speedy Gonzalez. I
am de heads of Alfredo García and Joaquín Murrieta.
I am de guy who told Elton John to grow some funk
of his own.

Now when I first got here people would say,
"Sorry what's de name? Facoondoe?"

"No mang, Fa-cun-do, Facundo."

"Wow, dat's a new one. Mind if I call you Fac?"

"No mang, mind if I call you shithead?"

So, you know, I had to come up with a more
Saxonical name. And I looked around for a long time
till I found one I liked. And when I found the one I
wanted I took it. I estole it actually from a TV
show—"Broken Badge" or something like that.

I go by the name Wideload McKennah now and
I get a lot more respect, ese.

SLIDE Wideload

I live in de border ... I live in de zone, de barrio
and I gotta move 'cause dat neighbourhood is going
to de dogs.

'Cause dere's a lot of yuppies moving in and
dey're wrecking de neighbourhood and making all
kinds of noise wif renovating and landscaping and
knocking down walls and comparing stained glass.

So I gotta move.

But first I gotta make some money—I want to
cash in on de Latino Boom. Ya, dere's a Latino
Boom, we are a very hot commodity right now. And
what I really want to do is get a big chunk of toxic
wasteland up on de Trans-Canada highway and make
like a third-world theme park.

You know, you drive up to like big barbed wire
gates with guards carrying sub-machine-guns and you

park your car and den a broken-down Mercedes Benz bus comes along and takes you in under guard, of course. And you can buy an International Monetary Fund Credit Card for fifty bucks and it gets you on all de rides.

And as soon as you're inside somebody steals your purse and a policeman shows up but he's totally incompetent and you have to bribe him in order to get any action. Den you walk through a slum on the edge of a swamp wif poor people selling tortillas. And maybe like a disappearing rain-forest section dat you can actually wander through and search for rare plants and maybe find de cure to cancer and maybe find ... Sean Connery ... and you rent little golf carts to drive through it and de golf cart is always breaking down and you have to fix it yourself. And while you're fixing de golf cart in de sweltering noonday sun a drug lord comes along in his hydrofoil and offers to take you to his villa where you can have lunch and watch a multi-media presentation on drug processing.

I figure it would do great—you people love dat kinda *shit*. I mean if de Maharishi can get a theme park going ... And I can also undercut dose travel agencies dat are selling package tours of Brazilian slums. Dis would be way cheaper, safer and it would generate a lot of jobs. For white people too. And I would make some money and be able to move out of the barrio and into Forest Hill.

Ya, a little house in Forest Hill. Nice neighbour-hood. Quiet. Good place to bring up like fifteen kids.

Course dis country is full of nice neighbourhoods—
Westmount in Montreal looks good, or Vancouver
you know, Point Grey is lovely or Kitsilano it's kind
of like de Beaches here in Toronto. Or de Annex—
mang, I love de Annex: you got professionals, you got
families, you got professional families. Ya I could live
dere. Hey mang, we could be neighbours—would
you like dat? Sure, I'm moving in next door to ... you
... and I'm going to wash my Mustang every day and
overhaul de engine and get some grease on de side-
walk and some friends like about twelve are gonna
come and stay with me for a few ... Years.

You like music? Goood!

Ya, how 'bout a Chicano for a neighbour? Liven
up de neighbourhood.

SLIDE Chicano: a person who drives a loud car that sits
low to the ground?
a kind of Mexican?
generic term for a working class Latino?
a wetback?
a Mexican born in Saxon America?

Technically, I don't qualify as a Chicano. I wasn't
born in East L.A. I wasn't born in de southwest
U.S.A. I wasn't even born in Méjico. Does dis make
me Hispanic?

SLIDE Hispanic: someone who speaks Spanish?
a Spaniard?
a Latino?
root of the word spic?

26

Dese terms, Latino, Hispanic, are very tricky you know, but dey are de only terms we have so we have to use dem wif caution. If you will indulge me for a moment I would like to make this point painfully clear:

De term Hispanic, for example, comes from the Roman word, Hispania, which refers to de Iberian peninsula or Espain. Espain is a country in Europe. Many people who today are referred to as Hispanic have nothin to do wif Hispain. Some of dem don't even speak Hispanish.

De term Latino is also confusing because it lumps a whole lot of different people into one category. Dere is a world of difference between de right wing Cubans living in Miami, exiled Salvadorean leftists, Mexican speakers of Nahuatl, Brazilian speakers of Portuguese, Ticos, Nuyoricans (dat's a Puerto Rican who lives in New York) and den dere's de Uruguayans—I mean dey're practically European ... As for me, let's just say ... I'm a pachuco.[3]

It Starts

VERDECCHIA Okay, I just want to stop for a second before we get all confused.

I've known that I've been lost for quite some time now—years and years—but if I can find the moment that I first discovered I was lost, there might be a clue ...

This all starts with Jorge. After I'd been in therapy for a few months, Jorge suggested I go see El Brujo. I wasn't keen on the idea, being both sceptical and afraid of things like curanderos, but Jorge was persuasive and lent me bus fare enough to get me at least as far as the border ...

It actually starts before that. It starts in France, Paris, France, the Moveable Feast, the City of Light, where I lived for a couple of years. En France où mes étudiants me disaient que je parlais le français comme une vache Catalan. En France où j'étais étranger, un anglais, un Argentin–Canadien, un faux touriste. Paris, France where I lived and worked illegally, where I would produce my transit pass whenever policemen asked for my papers. In France, where I was undocumented, extralegal, marginal and where for some reason, known perhaps only by Carlos Gardel and Julio Cortázar, I felt almost at home.

Or it starts before the City of Light, in the City of Sludge: Kitchener, Ontario. There in Kitchener, where I learned to drive, where I first had sex, where there was nothing to do but eat doughnuts and dream of elsewhere. There in Kitchener, where I once wrote a letter to the editor and suggested that it was not a good idea to ban books in schools, and it was there in Kitchener that a stranger responded to my letter and suggested that I go back to my own country.

No. It starts, in fact, at the airport where my parents and my grandparents and our friends couldn't stop crying and hugged each other continually and said goodbye again and again until the stewardess finally came and took me out of my father's arms and carried me on to the plane, forcing my parents to finally board—

Maybe. Maybe not.

Maybe it starts with Columbus. Maybe it starts with the genius Arab engineer who invented the rudder. Maybe a little history is required to put this all in order.

History

SLIDE An Idiosyncratic History of America

VERDECCHIA Our History begins approximately 200 million years ago in the Triassic Period of the Mesozoic Era when the original supercontinent Pangaea broke up and the continents of the earth assumed the shapes we now recognize.

SLIDE map of the world

5000 B.C.: The first settlements appear in the highlands of Mexico and in the Andes mountains.

1500 B.C.: The pyramid at Teotihuacán is built.

SLIDE photo of the pyramid

Early 1400's A.D.: Joan of Arc

SLIDE statue of Joan of Arc

29

is born and shortly thereafter, burned. At the same time, the Incas in Peru develop a highly efficient political system.

1492: Catholic Spain is very busy integrating the Moors. These Moors or Spaniards of Islamic culture who have been in Spain some 700 years suffer the same fate as the Spanish Jews: they are converted, or exiled, their heretical books and bodies burned.

SLIDE portrait of Christopher Columbus

Yes, also in 1492: this chubby guy sails the ocean blue.

1500: Pedro Cabral stumbles across what we now call Brazil— Portugal, fearing enemy attacks, discourages and suppresses writing about the colony.

1542: The Spanish Crown passes the Laws of the Indies. These Laws state that the settlers have only temporary concessions to these lands while the real owners are the Native Americans. Curiously, the Spanish Crown does not inform the Natives that the land is legally theirs. An oversight no doubt.

1588: The invincible Spanish Armada is defeated. Spain grows poorer and poorer as gold from the New World is melted down to pay for wars and imported manufactured goods from the developed northern countries. El Greco finishes *The Burial of Count Orgaz.*

SLIDE *The Burial of Count Orgaz*

Lope de Vega writes *La Dragontea.* Caldéron de La Barca and Velázquez are about to be born.

1808: Beethoven writes Symphonies 5 & 6. France

invades Spain and in the power vacuum wars of independence break out all over New Spain. Goya paints

SLIDE *Executions of the Citizens of Madrid*

Executions of the Citizens of Madrid.
    1812: Beethoven writes Symphonies 7 & 8 and a war breaks out in North America.
    1832: Britain occupies the Malvinas Islands and gives them the new, silly name of the Falklands.
    1846: The U.S. attacks Mexico.
    1863: France attacks Mexico and installs an Austrian as emperor.
    1867: Mexico's Austrian emperor is executed, volume one of *Das Kapital* is published and The Dominion of Canada is established.
    1902: Gorki writes *The Lower Depths,* the U.S. acquires control over the Panama Canal and Beatrix Potter writes *Peter Rabbit.*

SLIDE illustration from *Peter Rabbit*

    1961: Ernest Hemingway kills himself,

SLIDE photo of Ernest Hemingway

West Side Story

SLIDE photo of the "Sharks" in mid-dance

wins the Academy Award, a 680-pound giant sea bass is caught off the Florida coast,

31

SLIDE photo of large fish

and the U.S. attacks Cuba.

SLIDE photo of Fidel Castro

1969: Richard Nixon

SLIDE photo of Richard Nixon

is inaugurated as president of the U.S., Samuel Beckett

SLIDE photo of Samuel Beckett

is awarded the Nobel Prize for Literature, the Montreal Canadiens

SLIDE photo of the 1969 Canadiens team

win the Stanley Cup for hockey and I attend my first day of classes at Anne Hathaway Public School.

Roll Call

[*Music:* God Save the Queen]

VERDECCHIA I am seven years old. The teacher at the front of the green classroom reads names from a list.
"Jonathon Kramer?"
Jonathon puts his hand up. He is a big boy with

32

short red hair.

"Sandy Nemeth?"

Sandy puts her hand up. She is a small girl with long hair. When she smiles we can see the gap between her front teeth.

"Michael Uffelman?"

Michael puts his hand up. He is a tall boy with straight brown hair sitting very neatly in his chair.

My name is next.

Minutes, hours, a century passes as the teacher, Miss Wiseman, forces her mouth into shapes hitherto unknown to the human race as she attempts to pronounce my name.

"Gwillyou—ree—moo ... Verdeek—cheea?"

I put my hand up. I am a minuscule boy with ungovernable black hair, antennae and gills where everyone else has a mouth.

"You can call me Willy," I say. The antennae and gills disappear.

It could have been here—but I don't want to talk about myself all night.

Wideload's Terms

WIDELOAD Thank God.

I mean I doan know about you but I hate it when I go to el teatro to de theatre and I am espectin' to see a play and instead I just get some guy up dere talking about himself—deir life story—who cares? por favor ... And whatever happened to plays anyway—anybody remember plays? Like wif a plot and like a central character? Gone de way of modernism I guess and probaly a good thing too. I mean I doan know if I could stand to see another play about a king dat's been dead for 400 years—

Anyway—

The Smiths

WIDELOAD When I first got to América del Norte I needed a place to live and I diden have a lot of money so I stayed wif a family. The Smiths—Mr. and Mrs. and deir two kids Cindy and John. And it was nice you know. Like it was like my first contact with an ethnic family and I got a really good look at de way dey live. I mean sure at times it was a bit exotic for me, you know de food for example, but mostly I just realized they were a family like any other wif crazy aunts and fights and generation gaps and communication problems and two cars, a VCR, a microwave, a cellular phone and a dog named Buster dat ate my socks.

Dey wanted to know all about me so I told dem stories about my mafioso uncle El Gato and how he won a tank and his wife in a poker game, and stories about my aunt, the opera singer, Luisa la Sonrisa, and about my cousin, Esperanza, about her border crossings and how she almost fell in love.

I came here because I wanted some perspective— you know working for a mafioso gives you a very particular point of view about de world. You know, we all need a filter to look at de world through. Like standing in Latin America I get a clear view of

34

the early seventies, but reports persist of
ponsored assassinations, kidnappings and
me about it man, I saw *Missing*.)
now 1990 and the horrific Pinochet
a thing of the past. I ride a comfort-
Santiago and continue reading my
tunately, South America's democracies
higher street-crime rates than the police
it all depends on how you define street
out the window and read the graffiti:
ha no duerme. I count all the police-
block it seems. What was it like under
oliceman in every house?

Carlos Santana]

m a ten-hour flight, I check into the
Tito, listed on page 302 of your
oderate, small hotel with six suites,
ight singles, bar, homey atmosphere,
d on one of the main streets in Santiago
at Huérfanos 578. (Huérfanos—
rphans.) I shower, shave and take an

sts from the street wake me up and pul
dow.
ree storeys below, directly in front of
and homey Hotel de Don Tito, there
directly below my window, there a mar
hirt soaked an impossible red, lies
enormous crowd gathers. I reach for
d begin to take photographs. I take

Norteamérica and standing on Latin America while
living in Norf America gives me a new filter, a new
perspective. Anyway, it was time to change my filter
so I came here to estudy. Sí, thanks to mi tío El Gato
and my cousin Esperanza who always used to say,
"You should learn to use your brain or somebody else
will use it for you," I practically have a doctorate in
Chicano estudies. Dat's right—Chicano estudies ...
Well not exactly a doctorate, more like an M.A. or
most of an M.A., cause I got my credits all screwed
up and I diden finish—my professors said I was
ungovernable. I lacked discipline. You know instead
of like doing a paper on de historical roots of the
oppression of La Raza I organized an all-night Salsa
Dance Party Extravaganza. I also organized de
month-long "Chico and de Man" Memorial
Symposium which I dedicated to my cousin,
Esperanza, back home.

Going Home

VERDECCHIA   I had wanted to go home for many years
but the fear of military service in Argentina kept me
from buying that plane ticket. Nobody was certain
but everybody was pretty sure that I had committed
treason by not registering for my military service
when I was sixteen, even though I lived in Canada.
Everybody was also reasonably sure that I would be
eligible for military service until I was thirty-five.
And everybody was absolutely certain that the
minute I stepped off a plane in Buenos Aires, military

35

policemen would spring from the tarmac, arrest me and guide me to a jail cell where they would laugh at my earrings and give me a proper haircut.

I phoned the consulate one day to try to get the official perspective on my situation. I gave a false name and I explained that I wanted to go HOME for a visit, that I was now a Canadian citizen and no, I hadn't registered for my military service. The gentleman at the consulate couldn't tell me exactly what my status was but he suggested that I come down to the consulate where they would put me on a plane which would fly me directly to Buenos Aires where I would appear before a military tribunal who could tell me in no uncertain terms what my status actually was.

"Well I'll certainly consider that," I said.

And I waited seven years. And in those seven years, the military government is replaced by a civilian one and I decide I can wait no longer; I will risk a return HOME. I set off to discover the Southern Cone.

To minimize my risk I apply for a new Canadian passport which does not list my place of birth,

SLIDE passport photos

and I plan to fly first to Santiago, Chile and then cross the border in a bus that traverses the Andes and goes to Mendoza, Argentina.

After an absence of almost fifteen years I am going home. Going Home. I repeat the words softly to myself—my mantra: I Am Going Home—all will be resolved, dissolved, revealed, I will claim my place in the universe when I Go Home.

36

[*Music*

I
this. I
bough
friend
Spani
Mont
more
maître
savage
alone
years
Intern
down
Che a
black
whose
and sa
I

Santiag

VERDECCH

C
immed
and is
lent se
stylish
ty. My
Pinocl

37

than it did in
government-s
torture. (Tell

Well, it is
dictatorship i
able bus into
Fodor's: unfo
seem to have
states. I guess
crime. I look
Ojo! La derec
men, one per
Pinochet? A

[*Music*: Jingo

Tired fro
Hotel de Dor
Fodor's as a
eight twins, e
and it's locate
on Huérfano
Spanish for o
afternoon na

Three bl
me to the wi

There, t
the moderate
on the road,
in a suit, his
writhing as a
my camera a

38

photographs with a 135 mm. telephoto and then change lenses to get a sense of the crowd that has built up. I take photographs of the man who was shot on the first day of my return home after an absence of almost fifteen years, as more policemen arrive pulling weapons from their jean jackets. I take photographs as the man in the suit, his lower body apparently immobilized, reaches wildly for the legs that surround him, as the motorcycle police expertly push the crowd away from the Hotel de Don Tito, moderate in Fodor's, Huérfanos 578, homey, page 302. I take photographs as still more policemen arrive waving things that look like Uzis. I take photographs with a Pentax MX and a 35 mm. F 2.8 lens as the dying man, one of his shoes lying beside him, his gun on the road, gives up reaching for the legs around him. I take photographs from my room in the Hotel de Don Tito, Huérfanos 578, moderate in Fodor's, as the press arrives and NO AMBULANCE EVER COMES. I take photographs, 64 ASA Kodachromes, as he dies and I take photographs as the policemen (all men) talk to each other and I wonder if anyone has seen me and I take photographs as the policemen smoke cigarettes and cover him up and I take photographs and I realize that I have willed this to happen.

Dancing

WIDELOAD Oye, you know I do like you Saxons. Really, you guys are great. I always have a very good time whenever we get together. Like sometimes, I'll be out

39

with some friends from de Saxonian community and we'll be out at a bar having a few cervezas, you know, vacilando, and some music will be playing and *La Bamba* will come on. And all de Saxons get all excited and start tappin' deir toes and dey get all carried away and start doing dis thing with deir heads ... and dey get dis look in deir eyes like it's Christmas an dey look at me and say, "Hey Wideload, *La Bamba.*"

"Ya mang, la puta bamba."

"Wideload man, do you know de words?"

"Do I know de words?

"Mang, do I have an enorme pinga? Of course I know de words: pala pala pala la bamba ... Who doesn't know de words?"

[*Music:* Navidad Negra, *Ramiro's Latin Orchestra*]

Espeaking of music I haf to say dat I love de way you guys dance. I think you Saxons are some of de most interesting dancers on de planet. I lof to go down to the Bamboo when my friend Ramiro is playing and just watch you guys dance because you are so free—like nothing gets in your way: not de beat, not de rhythm, nothing.

What I especially like to watch is like a Saxon guy dancing wif a Latin woman. Like she is out dere and she's smiling and doing a little cu-bop step and she's having a good time and de Saxon guy is like trying really hard to keep up, you know he's making a big effort to move his hips independently of his legs and rib cage and he's flapping his arms like a flamenco dancer. Generally speaking dis applies just to the male Saxon—Saxon women seem to have learned a move or two …

Of course part of de problem is dat you guys wear very funny shoes for dancing—I mean like dose giant running shoes with built-in air compressors and padding and support for de ankles and nuclear laces—I mean you might as well try dancing wif snowshoes on. Your feet have got to be free, so dat your knees are free so dat your hips are free—so dat you can move your culo wif impunity.

So dere dey are dancing away: de Saxon guy and de Latin woman or de Saxon woman and de Latin guy and de Saxon, you can see de Saxon thinking:

Wow, he/she can really dance, he/she can really move those hips, he/she keeps smiling, I think he/she likes me, I bet he/she would be great in bed …

Now dis is important so I'm going to continue talking about it—even though it always gets real quiet whenever I start in on this stuff.

Now dere are two things at work here: the first is the fact that whenever a Latin and a Saxon have sex it is going to be a mind-expanding and culturally enriching experience porque nosotros sabemos hacer cosas que ni se imaginaron en la *Kama Sutra,* porque nosotros tenemos un ritmo, un calor un sabor un tumbao de timbales de conga de candomble de kilombo. Una onda, un un dos tres, un dos. Saben …?

Dat's de first factor at work and for dose of you who want a translation of dat come and see me after de show or ask one of de eSpanish espeakers in de audience at intermission.

De second component is the Exotica Factor. De

41

Latin Lover Fantasy. And I'll let you in on a little
secret: Latins are no sexier dan Saxons—well maybe
just a little. De difference is dis: we like it. A lot. And
we practise. A lot. Like we touch every chance we get.

Now I doan want you to get de impression I'm
picking on you Saxons. Nothing could be further
from my mind ... I have de greatest respect for your
culture ... and you know, every culture has its own
fertility dances, its own dance of sexual joy—you
people hab de Morris Dance,

SLIDE photo of Morris Dancers in mid-dance

and hey, you go to a Morris Dance Festival and it's de
Latinos who look silly. You have de Morris Dance—
very sexy dance—you know, a bunch of guys hop-
ping around wif bells on and every once in a while
swinging at each other. Now, I am not doing de
dance justice and I am looking for a Morris Dance
teacher so if you know of one please pass deir name
along. You have de Morris Dance and we have de
mambo, de rumba, de cumbia, de son, son-guajiro,
son-changui, de charanga, de merengue, de guaguan-
co, de tango, de samba, salsa ... shall I continue?

Latin Lover

WIDELOAD Latin Lovers.

SLIDE photo of Antonio Banderas

Dis is Antonio Banderas. He is a Spanish actor, a Spaniard from Spain. Dat's in Europe. Some of you may know him from Almódovar films like *Tie Me Up, Tie Me Down* and some of you may know him from de Madonna movie where he appears as de object of her desire and some of you may know him from *De Mambo Kings* based on de excellent book by Oscar Hijuelos. Now according to *Elle* magazine (and dey should know)

SLIDE *Elle* magazine cover

Antonio Banderas is de latest incarnation of de Latin Lover. It says right here: "Antonio Banderas—A Latin Love God Is Born."
    De Latin Lover is always being reincarnated. Sometimes de Latin Lover is a woman—Carmen Miranda for example.

SLIDE photo of Carmen Miranda

She was Brazilian. Poor Carmen, smiling, sexy even with all dose goddamned bananas on her head—do you know she ended up unemployable, blacklisted because a certain Senator named McCarthy found her obscene?

SLIDE photo of Delores Del Rio

Dere was also Delores Del Rio,

SLIDE photo of Maria Montez

Maria Montez, some of you may remember her as
Cobra Woman,

SLIDE photo of Rita Moreno

den Rita Moreno, today we have Sonia Braga ...

SLIDE photo of Sonia Braga

SLIDE photo of Rudolph Valentino

For de men dere was Rudolph Valentino,

SLIDE photo of Fernando Lamas

Fernando Lamas,

SLIDE photo of Ricardo Montalban

Mr. Maxwell House and of course ...

SLIDE photo of Desi Arnaz

Desi Arnaz whom we all remember as Ricky Ricardo
from Ricky and Lucy those all-time-great TV lovers.
Now Ricky may not exactly live up to de steamy
image of unbridled sexuality we expect from our
Latin Lovers but you have to admit he's a pretty pow-
erful icon. Funny, cute, musical and more often dan
not, ridiculous.

Let's see what *Elle* magazine has to say about
Latin Lovers:

"He's short dark and handsome, with lots of black hair from head to chest. He's wildly emotional, swinging from brooding sulks to raucous laughter and singing loudly in public. He's relentlessly romantic, with a fixation on love that looks to be total: he seems to be always about to shout, 'I must have you.'"

SLIDE I must have you.

"He is the Latin Lover, an archetype of masculinity built for pleasure."

The article begins by explaining the myth of the Latin Lover and then uses the myth to explain Banderas. Banderas cannot explain himself apparently because his English is too limited.

In *Mirabella*,

SLIDE *Mirabella* cover

another glossy magazine, there is another article on Banderas and it describes how Banderas pronounces the word LOVE. He pronounces it "Looov-aaa." Ooooh isn't dat sweet and sexy and don't you just want to wrap him up in your arms and let him whisper filthy things in your ear in Spanish and broken English? Especially when, as also described in the *Mirabella* article, he wipes his mouth on the tablecloth and asks, "What can I done?" Don't you just want to fuck him? I do. I wonder though if it would be quite so disarming or charming if it was Fidel Castro wiping his mouth on the tablecloth?

Dis is Armand Assante.

He plays Banderas's brother in de movie, *Mambo Kings*.

He is an Italo–American.

The subtitle here says *De Return of Macho*. Did macho go away for a while? I hadn't noticed. Anyway, it has returned for dose of you who missed it.

According to dis article in *GQ*, Signor Assante almost did not get de part in de movie because de estudio, Warner Brothers, wanted a name—dey wanted a big-name A-list actor—like Robin Williams to play a Cuban. But, according to de article the director of the movie had the "cajones"

SLIDE cajones

to buck the studio and give the part to Assante. Cajones …

Now the word I think they want to use is cojones,

SLIDE cojones

which is a colloquial term for testicles. What they've ended up with in *GQ* magazine is a sentence that means the director had the crates or boxes to buck the studio.

SLIDE cojones = testicles

SLIDE cajones = crates

46

Could be just a typo but you never know.

Now I find it really interesting dat all of the advance publicity for dis movie was concentrated in de fashion-magazine trade. When a Hollywood trade-magazine and major newspapers tell me de movie feels authentic and when the movie is pre-sold because its stars are sexy Latino love gods and macho and cause dey wear great clothes, I begin to suspect dat dis movie is another attempt to trade on the look, the feel, de surface of things Latin.

It goes back to this thing of Latin Lovers being archetypes of men and women built for pleasure. Whose pleasure mang? Your movie-going pleasure? The pleasure of de Fashion–Industrial–Hollywood complex? Think about it—

In dose movies we can't solve our own problems, we can't win a revolution without help from gringos, we can't build the pyramids at Chichén Itzá without help from space aliens, we don't win the Nobel Prize, no, instead we sing, we dance, we fuck like a dream, we die early on, we sleep a lot, we speak funny, we cheat on each other, we get scared easy, we amuse you. And its not just in de movies—it's in—

[A loud buzzer goes off]

Dere goes de buzzer—indicating dat some forty-five minutes of de show have elapsed and dat less dan fifteen minutes remain till intermission. Unofficial tests indicate dat audiences grow restless at de forty-five-minute mark so we are going to take de briefest of breaks and give you de opportunity to shift around

in your seats and scratch your culo and whisper to
the person next to you.

And during dis break we are gonna see some clips
from a mega-musical spectacular dat will be opening
here soon. It's called *Miss Tijuana*. Dey are gonna be
building a special theatre to house *Miss Tijuana* cause
it's a very big show wif lots of extras. It's going to be
an adobe theatre wif Adobe Sound.

Here's de break.

[*Video: clips of cartoons and movies featuring, among
other things: Latinos, Hispanics, dopey peasants,
Anthony Quinn and a certain mouse. Cheesy music
plays. Then the loud buzzer goes off again*]

Travel Sickness

VERDECCHIA When I travel I get sick. I've thrown up in
most of the major centres of the western world: Paris,
Rome, Madrid, New York, London, Venice, Seaforth,
Ontario, Calgary … And it's not just too much to
drink or drugs, sometimes it's as simple as the shape
of the clouds in the sky or the look on someone's face
in the market or the sound my shoes make on the
street. These things are enough to leave me shaking
and sweating in bed with a churning stomach, no
strength in my legs and unsettling dreams.

Well, I'm in Buenos Aires and so far I haven't
thrown up. So far, Everything's Fine.

We meet in Caballito. And Alberto and I have
dinner in a bright, noisy restaurant called The Little

48

Pigs and Everything's Fine. And now we're looking
for a place to hear some music, a place in San Telmo
to hear some contemporary music, not tango and not
folklore. Alberto wants to go see a band called Little
Balls of Ricotta and Everything's Fine, but first we
have to get the flat tire on his Fiat fixed. We stop at a
gomería, a word which translated literally would be a
"rubbery," it's a place where they fix tires. I'm feeling
like I need some air so I get out of the car and
Everything's Fine, I'm looking at Alberto in the
gomería there's this weird green light in the shop and
I'm leaning over the car and suddenly I feel very hot
and awful and just as quickly I suddenly feel better. I
wake up and I'm sitting on the road and somebody's
thrown up on me, then I realize the vomit is my own
and I'm in Buenos Aires and I'm sick and I've thrown
up and we're in a tricky part of town and the cops
will be passing by any minute and I haven't done my
military service—

Alberto puts me in the back of the car. From the
gomería, Alberto brings me half a Coke can whose
edges have been carefully trimmed and filed down—
a cup of water. I lie in the back of Alberto's uncle's
Fiat as we pull away. There's a knock at the window
and I'm sure it's the police saying, "Excuse me but
have you got a young man who hasn't done his military service in there, a degenerate who's vomited all
over the street?"—but no, it's the guy from the
gomería: he wants his Coke-can cup back.

We drive back to my apartment, not mine actually, my grandmother's, but she's not there for some
reason and I'm using it. I'm feeling a little better but

weak, can't raise my head, I watch Buenos Aires spin and speed past and around me, through the back window, like a movie I think, ya that's it, I'm in a Costa Gavras film.

I'm on the toilet in my grandmother's apartment, I leave tomorrow, back to Canada, and I ruined this last evening by getting sick, I can't fly like this all poisoned and I have to throw up again and the bidet is right there, and for some reason I remember Alberto telling me how by the end of the month people are coming to his store on the edge of the villa, on the edge of the slum, and asking if they can buy one egg or a quarter of a package of butter or a few cigarettes, and I think yes, in a few years we will kill for an apple, and I throw up in the bidet and I just want to go home—but I'm already there—aren't I? Eventually, I crawl into my grandmother's bed and sleep.

[*Music:* Asleep, *Astor Piazzolla and Kronos Quartet*]

I dream of Mount Aconcagua, of Iguaçú, of Ushuaia and condors, of the sierras yellow and green, of bay, orange, quebracho and ombu trees, of running, sweating horses, of café con crema served with little glasses of soda water, of the smell of Particulares 30, of the vineyards of Mendoza, of barrels full of ruby-red vino tinto, of gardens as beautiful as Andalusia in spring. I dream of thousands of emerald-green parrots flying alongside my airplane—parrots just like the ones that flew alongside the bus as I travelled through the interior.

The Other

VERDECCHIA I would like to clear up any possible mis-
impression. I should state now that I am something
of an impostor. A fake. What I mean is: I sometimes
confuse my tenses in Spanish. I couldn't dance a
tango to save my life.

All sides of the border have claimed and rejected
me. On all sides I have been asked: How long have
you been …? How old were you when …? When did
you leave? When did you arrive? As if it were somehow possible to locate on a map, on an airline sched-
ule, on a blueprint, the precise coordinates of the
spirit, of the psyche, of memory.

[*Music:* El Mal Dormido, *Atahualpa Yupanqui*]

As if we could somehow count or measure these
things.

These things cannot be measured—I know I tried.

I told the doctor: "I feel Different. I feel wrong,
out of place. I feel not nowhere, not neither."

The doctor said, "You're depressed."

I said, "Yes I am."

The doctor said, "Well …"

I said, "I want to be tested. Sample my blood,
scan my brain, search my organs. Find it."

"Find what?"

"Whatever it is."

"And when we find it?"

"Get rid of it."

They didn't find anything. Everything's absolutely normal, I was told. Everything's fine. Everything's where it should be. I wasn't fooled. I am a direct descendant of two people who once ate an armadillo—armadillo has a half-life of 2,000 years—you can't tell me that isn't in my bloodstream. Evita Perón once kissed my mother and that night she felt her cheek begin to rot. You can't tell me that hasn't altered my DNA.

El Teatro

WIDELOAD Okay,

[*The lights come up*]

let's see who's here, what's everybody wearing, let's see who came to El Teatro dis evening. What a good-looking bunch of people. What are you doing here tonight? I mean don't think we doan appreciate it, we do. We're glad you've chosen to come here instead of spending an evening in front of the Global Village Idiot Box.

Are you a Group? Do you know each other? No, well, some of you know de person next to you but collectively, you are strangers. Estrangers in de night. But perhaps by the end of the evening you will no longer be strangers because you will have shared an experience. You will have gone through dis show together and it will have created a common bond among you, a common reference point.

That's the theory anyway. That the theatre is valuable because a bunch of strangers come together and share an experience. But is it true? I mean how can you be sharing an experience when you are all (thankfully) different people? You have different jobs, different sexual orientations, different lives, different histories. You are all watching dis show from a different perspective. Most of you, for example, have been awake.

Maybe the only thing you have in common is dat you are all sitting here right now listening to me speculate about what you might have in common and dat you all paid sixteen dollars to hear me do so. But not everybody paid sixteen dollars, my friends get in free. So do theatre critics. Weird, huh?

People do end up in the weirdest places. I mean some of you are from Asia, some from el Caribe, some from Africa, some of you are from de Annex, and you ended up in dis small room with me. And me, I left home to escape poverty and I ended up working in de theatre? Weird. Let's take a break, huh?

It's intermission ladies and gentlemen. Get your hot chocolate and Wideload wine gums outside.

[*Music:* La Guacamaya, *Los Lobos*]

End of Act I

Act II

SLIDE Every North American, before this century is over,
will find that he or she has a personal frontier with
Latin America.
  This is a living frontier, which can be nourished by
information but, above all, by knowledge, by under-
standing, by the pursuit of enlightened self-interest
on both parts.
  Or it can be starved by suspicion, ghost stories,
arrogance, ignorance, scorn and violence.
— Carlos Fuentes[4]

[*Music:* Peligro, *Mano Negra*]

Call to Arms

VERDECCHIA [*voice-over*] This play is not a plea for toler-
  ance. This is not a special offer for free mambo
  lessons nor an invitation to order discount Paul
  Simon albums. This is a citation, a manifesto. This is
  a summons to begin negotiations, to claim your place
  on the continent.

Of Ferrets and Avocado

WIDELOAD NEVER GIVE A FERRET AVOCADO!

SLIDE photo of a ferret

De ferret ees a northern European animal—
known also as de polecat and related to de bear and
de wolberine. Dey are fierce little creatures, used to
kill pests like rabbits. De ferret can be domesticated.
Some of you may have a ferret of your own which
you have affectionately named Blinky or Squiggly or
Beowulf. Ferrets, as you ferret-owners will attest, are
excellent pets: Intelligent, playful, affectionate, cute
as all-get-out. It takes four generations to domesticate
a ferret but only one generation for the ferret to
revert to a feral state—dat means to go savage.
Interesting, huh?

De avocado is a fruit from de southern hemi-
sphere—known variously as avocado, aguacate and,
for some reason known only to themselves, as palta to
Argentinians. De avocado is a rich, nutritious fruit
which can be used in all sorts of ways—as a mayon-
naise, in guacamole, spread some on some pork ten-
derloin for a sanwich Cubano. Avocados make lousy
pets. Dey are not playful and do not respond at all to
commands.

Never give a ferret avocado.

Because it will blow up. Deir northern constitu-
tions cannot process de rich southern fruit.

Think about dat.

WIDELOAD I want to draw some attention to myself. Some more attention. I want to talk about dat nasty "S" word: Estereotype. I would like to set the record straight on dis subject and state dat I am by no means an estereotype. At least I am no more of an estereotype dan dat other person in de show: dat neurotic Argentinian. And I know dere's a lot of confusion on dis subject so let me offer a few pointers. If I was a real estereotype, I wouldn't be aware of it. I wouldn't be talking to you about being an estereotype.

If I was a real estereotype, you would be laughing at me, not with me.

And if I was a real estereotype, you wouldn't take me seriously and you do take me seriously. Don't you?

I'm the real thing. Don't be fooled by imitations.

Border Crossings

VERDECCHIA [*speaking to Customs Agent*] "Los Angeles. Uh, Los, Las Anngel— Lows Anjelees, uh, L.A.

"Two weeks.

"Pleasure.

"I'm a Canadian citizen.

"Pleasure." [*to audience*] Didn't I just answer that question?

[*to Customs Agent*] "I'm ... an ... actor actually.

"Ever seen 'Street Legal'?

"Well, I'm mostly in the theatre. I don't think ... Okay uh, the Tarragon uh, Canadian Stage, the—

"I'm not surprised.

"Yes, that's my book. Well, it's not *mine*. It's a novel. That I'm reading."

[*to audience*] Oh, Jeeezzuz. [*to Customs Agent*] "A guy, you know, who has a kind of identity problem and uh—

"I told you: pleasure. Come on what is this? I'm a Canadian citizen—we're supposed to be friends. You know, Free Trade, the longest undefended border in the world ... all that?" [*to audience*] I had less trouble getting into Argentina.

[*to Customs Agent*] "No, I'm not unemployed. I'm an actor. I'm between jobs, I'm on holidays

"Thanks."

[*to audience*] Some borders are easier to cross than others. Try starting a conversation in Vancouver with the following statement: "I like Toronto."

Some things get across borders easier than others.

SLIDE large, angry bee

Killer bees for example.

[*Music:* Muiñeira de Vilanova, *Milladoiro*]

Music. Music crosses borders.

My grandfather was a gallego, from Galicia, Spain. This music is from Galicia and yes, those are bagpipes. Those of us with an ethnomusicological bent can only ask ourselves, "How did the bagpipes ever end up in ... Scotland?"

Ponte guapa que traen el haggis!

The bandoneon, cousin to the concertina and stepbrother to the accordion, came to the Río de la Plata via Germany. Originally intended for organless churches, the bandoneon found its true calling in the whore-houses of Buenos Aires and Montevideo playing the most profane music of all: the tango.

Banned by Pope Pius X, the tango was, at first, often danced only by men because its postures were considered too crude, too sexual for women—it was after all, one of the first dances in which men and women embraced.

King Ludwig of Bavaria forbade his officers to dance it, and the Duchess of Norfolk explained that the tango was contrary to English character and manners, but the tango, graciously received in the salons of Paris, soon swept London's Hotel Savoy and the rest of Europe. Finally, even polite society in Argentina acknowledged it.

The tango, however, has not been entirely domesticated. It is impossible to shop or aerobicize to tango … porque el tango es un sentimiento que se baila.

And what is it about the tango, this national treasure that some say was born of the gaucho's crude attempts to waltz?

[*Music:* Verano Porteño, *Astor Piazzolla*][5]

It is music for exile, for the preparations, the significations of departure, for the symptoms of migration. It is the languishing music of picking through your belongings and deciding what to take.

It is the two a.m. music of smelling and caressing books none of which you can carry—books you leave behind with friends who say they'll always be here when you want them when you need them—music for a bowl of apples sitting on your table, apples you have not yet eaten, apples you cannot take—you know they have apples there in that other place but not these apples, not apples like these— You eat your last native apple and stare at what your life is reduced to—all the things you can stick into a sack. It will be cold, you will need boots, you don't own boots except these rubber ones—will they do? You pack them, you pack a letter from a friend so you will not feel too alone.

Music for final goodbyes for one last drink and a quick hug as you cram your cigarettes into your pocket and run to the bus, you run, run, your chest heaves, like the bellows of the bandoneon. You try to watch intently to emblazon in your mind these streets, these corners, those houses, the people, the smells, even the lurching bus fills you with a kind of stupid happiness and regret— Music for the things you left behind in that room: a dress, magazines, some drawings, two pairs of shoes and blouses too old to be worn any more ... four perfect apples.

Music for cold nights under incomprehensible stars, for cups of coffee and cigarette smoke, for a long walk by the river where you might be alone or you might meet someone. It is music for encounters in shabby stairways, the music of lovemaking in a narrow bed, the tendernesses, the caress, the pull of strong arms and legs.

Music for men and women thin as bones.

Music for your invisibility.

Music for a letter that arrives telling you that he is very sick. Music for your arms that ache from longing from wishing he might be standing at the top of the stairs waiting to take the bags and then lean over and kiss you and even his silly stubble scratching your cold face would be welcome and you only discover that you're crying when you try to find your keys—

Music for a day in the fall when you buy a new coat and think perhaps you will live here for the rest of your life, perhaps it will be possible, you have changed so much, would they recognize you? would you recognize your country? would you recognize yourself?

WIDELOAD Basically, tango is music for fucked-up people.

VERDECCHIA Other things cross borders easily. Diseases and disorders. Like amnesia. Amnesia crosses borders.

Drug War Deconstruction

WIDELOAD Hey, I want to show you a little movie. It's a home movie. It came into my home and I saved it to share with my friends. It's called *The War On Drugs*. Some of you may have seen it already so we are just gonna see some of de highlights.

[*An edited drug-war TV movie plays without sound.* WIDELOAD *explains the action*]

60

Dis is de title: It says DE WAR ON DRUGS. In BIG BLOCK LETTERS. In English. Dis is another title: *The Cocaine Cartel*. Dey're talking about de Medellin Cartel in Colombia.

Dis is de hero. He is a Drug Enforcement Agent from de U.S. who is sent to Colombia to take on de Medellin Cartel. He is smiling. He kisses his ex-wife. [*as character on-screen turns away*] Oh ... he is shy.

Dis woman is a kind of judge, a Colombian judge, and she agrees to prosecute de Medellin Cartel, to build a case against de drug lords even though her life is being threatened here on de phone even as we watch. Watch. [*on-screen, the judge speaks into the phone;* WIDELOAD *provides the dialogue*] "But ... I didn't order a pizza."

Dis guy is a jounalist, an editor for a big Colombian newspaper. He is outspoken in his criticism of the drug lords. He has written editorial after editorial condemning de Cartel and calling for de arrest of de drug lords. He is a family man, as we can tell by his Volvo car and by de presents which he loads into de car to take to his loved ones.

Okay, dis is a long shot so can we fast-forward through this part?

[*The tape speeds up*]

He's going home after a hard day at de office. He is in traffic. He is being followed by two guys on a motorcycle. Dey come to an intersection.

[*The tape resumes normal speed*]

Dey estop. De light is red. De guy gets off de motorcycle. Dum-dee-bumbe-dum. He has a gun! Oooh! And de family-man editor is killed, and as we can see he is driving one of dose Volvos wif de built-in safety feature dat when de driver is killed, de car parks itself automatically. Very good cars Volvos.

Dis is de Medellin Cartel. Dese are de drug lords. Dey are de bad guys. We know dey are bad because dey have manicured hands, expensive jewellery, even more expensive suits and ... dark hair. Dere's a lot of dem, dey are at a meeting, talking business. And dis guy is de kingpin, Pablo Escobar, head of de Medellin Cartel, de baddest of de bad. We know he is bad because he has reptilian eyes.

Okay, lemme put dis on pause for a second—Dis movie shows us a lot of things. It shows us dat drugs wreck families: in dis case de family of de nice white guy who is trying to stop de drug dealers—nobody in his family uses drugs—it's just he spends so much time fighting drugs dat his family falls apart.

De movie shows us dat de drug lords are nasty people who will not hesitate to kill anybody who gets in deir way. And you all know dat de kingpin, Pablo Escobar isnow dead. But did you know dat Señor Escobar was one of the richest men in de world according to *The Economist* magazine? Now Señor Escobar was not only a giant in free-market capitalism, he was also very big in public works, especially public housing. Interesting, huh? De movie doesn't show us dat.

What else doesn't de movie show us?

It does not show us for example dat profits from de sale of cocaine are used to fund wars like de U.S. war on Nicaragua which left some 20,000 Nicaraguans dead. Dis movie does not show us dat right-wing Miami-based terrorists, major U.S. drug traffickers, de Medellin Cartel, Syrian drug and arms dealers, de CIA, de State Department and Oliver North all worked together to wage war on Nicaragua. It does not show us that charges against major U.S. drug traffickers—dose are de people who bring de drugs on to dis part of de continent—charges against dose people were dropped once they became involved in the Contra war against Nicaragua.

Some of you are, naturally, sceptical, and some of you have heard all dis before because you have read de Kerry Sub-Committee report. Allow me to recommend it to those of you who haven't read it. It is incomplete at 400 pages but it does outline dese things I'm talking about. It makes excellen' bedtime or bathroom reading. I urge you to pick up a copy. And if you have any questions gimme a call.

So de next time a blatant piece of propaganda like dis one comes on, I hope we will watch it sceptically, and de next time we stick a straw up our nose I hope we will take a moment to make sure we know exactly where de money we give our dealer is going.[6]

Audition

VERDECCHIA It's two o'clock on a wintry afternoon and I have an audition for a TV movie.

[A dialect tape plays]

The office has sliding glass doors, hidden lighting fixtures and extravagant windows. There are four or five people seated behind a table including a guy with very expensive sunglasses.

[**VERDECCHIA** *sits down in front of a video camera. A close-up of* **VERDECCHIA** *appears on a monitor. In the following section, he sometimes speaks to the camera and sometimes off-camera to the audience*]

[*on-camera*] Hi, I'm Guillermo Verdecchia. I'm with Noble Talent.
[*off-camera*] For those of you who aren't in the business this is called slating. And when I say the Business I do mean the Industry. Slating is the first thing you do when you audition for a part on a TV show or a movie—you put your face and your name and your agent's name on tape before you read the scene.
[*on-camera*] I'm 5'9". On a good day.
[*off-camera*] That's called a little joke. Always good to get the producers and director laughing.
[*on-camera*] I'm from Argentina, actually. My special skills include driving heavy machinery, tango-dancing, scuba-diving, polo-playing and badminton. I speak three languages including English and I specialize in El Salvadorean refugees, Italian bob-sledders, Arab horse-thieves and Uruguayan rugby-players who are forced to cannibalize their friends when their plane crashes in the Andes.

[*off-camera*] Actually, I've never played a horse-thief or a rugby cannibal but I have auditioned for them an awful lot.

[*on-camera*] No. I've never been on "Really—True—Things—That—Actual—Cops—Do—As—Captured—By—Totally—Average—Citizens—With—Only—A—Video—Camera" before. It's a pleasure to be here. I'm reading for the part of Sharko.

[*off-camera*] An overweight Hispanic in a dirty suit it says here. I'm perfect for it.

[*on-camera*] Here we go.

[*Music:* Speedy Gonzalez Meets Two Crows From Tacos, *Carl Stalling*]

[*reads on-camera*] A black Camaro slides into the foreground, the engine throbbing like a hard-on from hell. Cut to close-up on trunk opening to reveal a deadly assault rifle. We hear Sharko's voice.

[VERDECCHIA *slips on a red bandanna*]

That's me.

[*reads Sharko's part on-camera*] There it is man. Is a thing of great beauty, no?

Sure man, I got what you ordered: silencer, bullets. I even got you a little extra cause I like doing business with you. A shiny new handgun.

Come on man, it's like brand-new. I got it off some old bag who used it to scare away peeping Toms.

Ah man, you take all this stuff for two grand, and I'll throw in the pistol for a couple of hundred. If you don't like it, you can sell it to some schoolkids for twice the price.

You already got one, hah? It was a present ... I see. A present from who?

From your Uncle Sam. Dat's nice. I diden know you had got an Uncle ...

[*with dawning horror*] You're a cop?

[*no longer reading; off-camera*] Well that's that. I should've done it differently. I could've been funnier.

[*on-camera*] Uh, would you like me to do the scene again? I could do it differently. I have a blue bandanna.

Okay. Thanks very much.

Nice to meet you.

SLIDE Ay ay ay ay I am the Frito Bandito

[*Music:* Cielito Lindo, *Placido Domingo*]

Santiago Two

VERDECCHIA I went back to Santiago and looked for some sign of the man who had been shot on the first day of my return. I looked for a stain, a scrape, anything, his shoe perhaps had been left behind. Nothing.

I wondered who he might have been. I remembered the redness of his shirt, the brightness of the sun. It was five o'clock.

A las cinco de la tarde.
Eran las cinco en punto de la tarde.
Un niño trajo la blanca sábana
a las cinco de la tarde.[7]

I saw someone die, I watched him die—that's what it looks like. That's where they end up—gun men, bank robbers, criminals and those brave revolutionaries and guerrillas you dreamed of and imagined you might be, might have been—they end up bleeding in the middle of the street, begging for water.

They end up dying alone on the hot pavement in a cheap suit with only one shoe. People die like that here. Ridiculous, absurd, pathetic deaths.

I came for a sign, I came because I had to know and now I know.

SLIDE photos of shooting

¡Que no quiero verla!
Que mi recuerdo se quema.
¡Avisad a los jazmines
con su blancura pequeña!
¡Que no quiero verla![8]

At the hotel they told me he was a bank robber. The papers said the same thing—a bank robber, died almost immediately in a shoot-out, name of Fernando Ochoa, nationality unknown, not interested. Case closed, dead gone erased.

I told them I was a Canadian writer/journalist/ filmmaker. They believed me. They let me look at the files, they let me talk, very briefly, to the cops who shot him, and since no one had shown up to claim them, they let me go through his personal effects. There wasn't much. A Bic lighter, with a tiny screw in the bottom of it so it could be refilled, an empty wallet. A package of Marlboros, with two crumpled cigarettes. There was a letter to someone named Mercedes. It read: "Querida Mercedes: It is bitterly cold tonight in my little room but I can look out the window and see the stars. I imagine that you are looking at them too. I take comfort in the fact that you and Ines and I share the same sky." There was also a newspaper from August 2nd, the day I arrived, the day he was shot. The headline claimed that former President Pinochet and the former Minister of the Interior knew nothing about the bodies that had been found in the Río Mapocho. I asked about his shoe—the one I saw on the road—no one knew anything about a shoe although they knew he wore size forty-two just like me—

Decompression

VERDECCHIA I'm sitting in the bar at Ezeiza, I'm in the bar at Heathrow, in the bar at Terminal sixty-two at LAX and I'm decompressing, preparing to surface. I'll arrive at Pearson at Mirabelle at Calgary International and I know that nothing will have changed and that everything will be different. I know that I've left some things behind—a sock in a hotel in Mendoza, a ring in a slum in Buenos Aires, a Zippo lighter in a lobby in Chile, a toenail in Ben's studio in Pougnadoresse, a combful of hair in the sink in the washroom at Florian in Venice.

These vestiges, these cells are slowly crawling towards each other. They are crossing oceans and mountains and six-lane expressways. They are calling to each other and arranging to meet in my sleep.

The Therapist

VERDECCHIA So ... I went to see a Therapist. He trained in Vienna but his office was in North York. I didn't tell him that I was afraid my toenails were coming after me in my sleep—I told him how I felt, what was happening. I have memories of things that never happened to me—I feel nostalgia for things I never knew—I feel connected to things I have no connection with, responsible, involved, implicated in things that happen thousands of miles away.

My Therapist asked about my family. If I'd been breast-fed. He asked about my sex life, my habits. He asked me to make a list of recurring dreams, a list of traumatic events including things like automobile accidents. I answered his questions and showed him drawings.

SLIDES drawings

My Therapist told me I was making progress. I believed him. (Who wouldn't believe a Therapist trained in Vienna?) At about the same time that I started doing what he called "deep therapy work," or

69

what I privately called reclaiming my inner whale, I
began to lose feeling in my extremities. It started as a
tingling in the tips of my fingers and then my hands
went numb. Eventually, over a period of months, I
lost all feeling in my left arm and I could hardly lift it.

My Therapist told me to see a Doctor.

The Doctor told me to rest and gave me pills.

Jorge made me go see El Brujo.

I said, "Jorge, what do you mean brujo? I'm not
going to somebody who's gonna make me eat seaweed."

Jorge said, "No, che loco, por favor, dejate de joder,
vamos che, tomate un matecito loco y vamos …"

Who could argue with that? "Where is this
Brujo, Jorge?"

"En la frontera."

"Where?"

"Bloor and Madison."

El Brujo

[*Music:* Mojotorro, *Dino Saluzzi*]

SLIDE The West is no longer west. The old binary models
   have been replaced by a border dialectic of ongoing
   flux. We now inhabit a social universe in constant
   motion, a moving cartography with a floating culture
   and a fluctuating sense of self.
   — Guillermo Gómez-Peña[9]

VERDECCHIA Porque los recién llegados me sospechan,
   porque I speak mejor Inglish que eSpanish,

porque mis padres no me creen,
porque no como tripa porque no como lengua,
porque hasta mis dreams are subtitled.

I went to see El Brujo at his place on Madison,
and you know I'd been to see a palm reader before so
I sort of knew what to expect. And he's this normal
guy who looks sort of like Freddy Prince except with
longer hair. And I told him about my Therapist and
about the numbness in my body and El Brujo said,
"He tried to steal your soul," and I laughed this kind
of honking sputtering laugh. I thought maybe he was
kidding.

El Brujo asked me, "How do you feel?" and I
said, "Okay. My stomach is kind of upset."

And he said, "Yes it is," and I thought oh please
just let me get back to reclaiming my inner whale.

El Brujo said, "You have a very bad border wound."

"I do?"

"Yes," he said, "and here in Mexico any border
wounds or afflictions are easily aggravated."

I didn't have the heart to tell him that we were at
Bloor and Madison in Toronto. El Brujo brought out
a bottle and thinking this would be one way to get
my money's worth, I started to drink.

El Brujo said, "I remember the night Bolívar
burned with fever and realized there was no way back
to the capital; the night he burned his medals and
cried, 'Whosoever works for the revolution ploughs
the seas.'"

"You *remember* that do you?" I said. "That was
what 1830 or something?" And I laughed and had
another drink. And El Brujo laughed too and we had

another drink and another drink and another.

El Brujo said, "I remember the Zoot Suit Riots. We were beat up for our pointy shoes and fancy clothes. I still have the scar." And he lifted up his shirt and showed me a gash. It was ugly and ragged and spotted with freshly dried blood. And that's when I first suspected that maybe we weren't at Bloor and Madison. You see, the Zoot Suit Riots were in 1943.

"What do you remember?" he asked.

"Not much."

"Try."

"I remember the Alamo?"

"No you don't."

"No, you're right I don't."

El Brujo said, "Your head aches."

"Yes it does."

"Because your left shoe is too tight. Why don't we burn it?" And maybe because I was drunk already, or maybe because I really thought that burning my shoe would help my headache, we threw it in the bathtub, doused it in lighter fluid and watched it burn this wild yellow and a weird green when the plastic caught on.

"What do you remember now?" he asked.

"I remember the French invasion of Mexico; I remember the Pastry War.

"I remember a bar of soap I had when I was little and it was shaped like a bear or a bunny and when it got wet, it grew hair, it got all fuzzy.

"I remember a little boy in a red snowsuit who ran away whenever anyone spoke to me in English. I remember la machine queso.

"I remember a gang of boys who wanted to steal my leather jacket even though we all spoke Spanish, a gang of boys who taught me I could be a long-lost son one minute and a tourist the next.

"I remember an audition where I was asked to betray and insult everything I claim to believe in and I remember that I did as I was asked.

"I remember practising t'ai chi in the park and being interrupted by a guy who wanted to start a fight and I remember thinking, 'Stupid drunken Mexican.' I remember my fear, I taste and smell my fear, my fear of young men who speak Spanish in the darkness of the park, and I know that somewhere in my traitorous heart I can't stand people I claim are my brothers. I don't know who did this to me. I remember feeling sick, I remember howling in the face of my fear ...

"I remember that I had dreamt I was playing an accordion, playing something improvised, which my grandmother recognized after only three notes as a tango from her childhood, playing a tango I had never learned, playing something improvised, not knowing where my fingers were going, playing an accordion, a tango which left me shaking and sweating.

"And I remember that I dreamt that dream one night after a party with some Spaniards who kept asking me where I was from and why my Spanish was so funny and I remember that I remembered that dream the first time one afternoon in Paris while staring at an accordion in a stall at the flea market and then found 100 francs on the street."

As I passed out El Brujo said, "The Border is your …"

[*Music:* Nocturno A Mi Barrio, *Anibal Troilo*]

SLIDE Cuándo, cuándo me fui?

The Other America

VERDECCHIA The airport is clean clean clean. And big big big. The car that takes me back into the city is big and clean. We drive through big clean empty land under a big, fairly clean sky. I'm back in Canada. It's nice. I'm back in Canada … oh well …

Why did I come back here?

This is where I work I tell myself, this is where I make the most sense, in this Noah's ark of a nation.

I reach into my pocket expecting to find my Zippo lighter and my last package of Particulares, but instead I find a Bic lighter with a tiny screw in the bottom of it so it can be refilled and a package of Marlboros with two crumpled cigarettes in it. And written on the package is a note, a quote I hadn't noticed before. It says:

No estoy en el crucero:
elegir
es equivocarse.[10]

SLIDE I am not at the crossroads:
to choose
is to go wrong.

74

And then I remember, I remember what El Brujo said, he said, "The Border is your Home."
I'm not in Canada; I'm not in Argentina.
I'm on the Border.
I am Home.
Mais zooot alors, je comprends maintenant, mais oui, merde! Je suis Argentin–Canadien! I am a post-Porteño neo-Latino Canadian! I am the Pan-American highway!

Latin Invasion

WIDELOAD It's okay, mang. Everybody relax. I'm back.
Ya, I been lying low in dis act but let me tell you I'm here to stay.
And it's quiz time. Please cast your memories way back and tell me who remembers José Imanez?
Ah-ha.
Who remembers de Frito Bandito? Who remembers Cheech and Chong?
Who remembers de U.S. invasion of Panama?
Dat's okay, dat was a trick question.
Who remembers de musical *De Kiss of de Spider Woman*? I do because I paid forty-two bucks to see it: a glamorous musical celebration of the torture and repression of poor people in a far-away place called Latin America where just over the walls of the prison there are gypsies and bullfights, women with big busts and all sorts of exotic, hot-blooded delights.

Dat's one of de hit songs from de show—*Big Busted Women*, some of you may recall ...

Who remembers de ad dat McDonald's had for deir fajitas not too long ago, featuring a guy called Pedro or Juan, and he says dat he's up here to get some McFajitas because [*reciting with supreme nasality*] "Dese are de most gueno fajitas I eber ate." What de fuck ees dat?

Can you imagine an ad dat went like: "Hey Sambo, what are you doing here?"

"Well, Mistah, I come up here to get some o' yo' pow'ful good McGrits. Mmmmm-mmm. Wif a watahmelon slice fo' deesert. Yassee."

I mean, we would be offended.

So, what is it with you people? Who do you think you are? Who do you think we are?

Yes, I am calling you you—I am generalizing, I am reducing you all to de lowest common denominator, I am painting you all with the same brush. Is it starting to bug you yet?

Of course, it is possible dat it doesn't really matter what I say. Because it's all been kind of funny dis evening.

Dat has been my mistake. I have wanted you to like me so I've been a funny guy.

[*Silence*]

Esto, en serio ahora—

Señoras y señores, we are re-drawing the map of America because economics, I'm told, knows no borders.

arguing that Piazzolla destroyed the tango. I would respond that Piazzolla re-invented and thereby rescued the tango from obsolescence. There is no forseeable end to this argument.

6. For a thorough analysis of the actual parameters of the War on Drugs, see Peter Dale Scott and Jonathan Marshall, *Cocaine Politics* (Berkeley: University of California Press, 1991). See also Noam Chomsky, *Deterring Democracy* (London: Verso, 1991).

7. Federico García Lorca, "La cogida y la muerte," in *Poema del cante jondo/Llanto por Ignacio Sánchez Mejías* (Buenos Aires: Editorial Losada, 1948), 145.

8. Federico García Lorca, "La sangre derramada," in *Poema del cante jondo/Llanto por Ignacio Sánchez Mejías* (Buenos Aires: Editorial Losada, 1948), 148.

9. Guillermo Gómez-Peña, "The World According to Guillermo Gómez-Peña," *High Performance* vol. 14, no. 3 (Fall 1991): 20. A MacArthur Fellow, Gómez-Peña has been a vital contributor to the U.S. debate on "multiculturalism," urging a rigorous appraisal of terms such as assimilation, hybridization, border-culture, pluralism and coexistence. A former member of Border Arts Workshop, he continues to explore notions of identity and otherness in his writings, and in performances such as *Border Brujo* and *The Year of the White Bear,* a collaboration with Coco Fusco.

10. Ocatvio Paz, "A la mitad de esta frase," in *A Draft of Shadows,* edited and translated by Eliot Weinberger (New York: New Directions, 1979), 72.

SLIDE Somehow the word "foreign" seems foreign these days. The world is smaller, so people are thinking bigger, beyond borders.
— IBM advertisement

Free Trade all de way from Méjico to Chile—dis is a big deal and I want to say dat it is a very complicated thing and it is only the beginning. And I wish to remind you, at this crucial juncture in our shared geographies, dat under dose funny voices and under dose funny images of de Frito Bandito and under all this talk of Money and Markets there are living, breathing, dreaming men, women and children.

I want to ask you please to throw out the metaphor of Latin America as North America's "backyard" because your backyard is now a border and the metaphor is now made flesh. Mira, I am in your backyard. I live next door, I live upstairs, I live across de street. It's me, your neighbour, your dance partner.

SLIDE Towards un futuro post-Columbian

Consider

WIDELOAD & VERDECCHIA Consider those come from the plains, del litoral, from the steppes, from the desert, from the savannah, from the Fens, from the sertão, from the rain forest, from the sierras, from the hills and high places.

Consider those come from the many corners of the globe to Fort MacMurray, to Montreal, to Saint

John's to build, to teach, to navigate ships, to weave, to stay, to remember, to dream.

Consider those here first. Consider those I have not considered. Consider your parents, consider your grandparents.

Consider the country. Consider the continent. Consider the border.

Going Forward

VERDECCHIA I am learning to live the border. I have called off the Border Patrol. I am a hyphenated person but I am not falling apart, I am putting together. I am building a house on the border.

And you? Did you change your name somewhere along the way? Does a part of you live hundreds or thousands of kilometres away? Do you have two countries, two memories? Do you have a border zone?

Will you call off the Border Patrol?

Ladies and gentlemen, please reset your watches. It is now almost ten o'clock on a Friday night—we still have time. We can go forward. Towards the centre, towards the border.

WIDELOAD And let the dancing begin!

[*Music:* El Jako, *Mano Negra*]

End

Endnotes

1. Carlos Fuentes, *Latin America: At War with th* (Toronto: CBC Enterprises, 1985), 8. This 1984 Massey L elegantly explores, in great detail, the divisions expressed b Mexico–North America border. Although Fuentes foc almost exclusively on the U.S., his analysis and insights pro a useful perspective for Canadians.

2. William Langewiesche, "The Border," *The Atlantic* vol. 26 no. 5 (May 1992): 56. This excellent article deals specifically wit the Mexico–U.S. border: border crossings, the Border Patrol drug traffic, economics, etc.

3. The term Latino has its shortcomings but seems to me more inclusive than the term Hispanic. Hispanic—which comes from Hispania, the Roman word for the Iberian peninsula—is a term used in the U.S. for bureaucratic, demographic, ideological and commercial purposes. Chicano refers to something else again. Chicano identity, if I may be so bold, is based in the tension of the border. Neither Mexicans nor U.S. Americans, Chicanos synthesize to varying degrees Mexican culture and language—including its Indigenous roots—and Anglo-American culture and language. Originally springing from the southwest U.S., Chicanos can be found all over, in Texas, in California, in New Mexico (!), in Detroit, maybe even in Canada. Chicanos speak a variety of regional tongues including formal or standard English and Spanish, North Mexican Spanish, Tex-Mex or Spanglish and even some caló or pachuco slang. See Gloria Anzaldúa's essay "How To Tame A Wild Tongue," in *Out There: Marginalization and Contemporary Culture* (New York and Cambridge, MA: The New Museum of Contemporary Art and M.I.T. Press, 1990), 203-211. Also of interest are the writing of Ron Arias, the poetry of Juan Felipe Herrera and the conjunto grooves of Steve Jordan.

4. Carlos Fuentes, *Latin America: At War with the Past* (Toronto: CBC Enterprises, 1985), 8.

5. Strictly speaking, Piazzolla's music is not tango with a capital T. Many purists would hotly contest my choice of music here,